Toronto
Maple Leafs

Written by
Don Cruickshank

Published by Weigl Educational Publishers Limited
6325 – 10 Street SE
Calgary, Alberta, Canada
T2H 2Z9

Web site: www.weigl.com

Library and Archives Canada Cataloguing in Publication

Cruickshank, Don
        Toronto Maple Leafs / Don Cruickshank.

(Hockey in Canada)
Includes index.
ISBN 1-55388-266-0 (bound)
ISBN 1-55388-267-9 (pbk.)

        1. Toronto Maple Leafs (Hockey team)--Juvenile literature.
I. Title. II. Series.

GV848.T6C78 2006   j796.962'6409713541   C2006-902129-5

Printed in the United States of America
1 2 3 4 5 6 7 8 9 0 10 09 08 07 06

Editor
Frances Purslow

Design and Layout
Terry Paulhus

Photo Credits
Hockey Hall of Fame: pages 3, 4R, 6, 11, 13, 19, 28.

We gratefully acknowledge the financial support of the Government of Canada through the Book Publishing Industry Development Program (BPIDP) for our publishing activities.

Contents

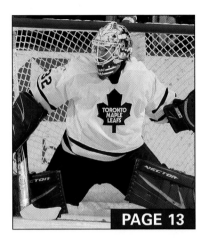

PAGE 13

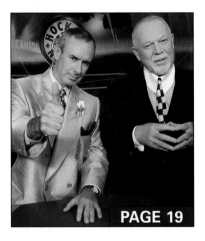

PAGE 19

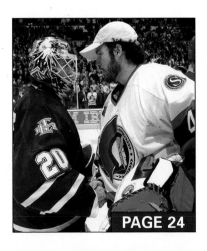

PAGE 24

The History of the NHL

ockey has been around for many years. Most historians credit James Creighton, a Canadian, with writing the first set of rules for hockey. These rules, called the Halifax Rules, are in the **Hockey Hall of Fame** in Toronto. In 1875, Creighton organized and played in the first official game of ice hockey using these rules. It was played at the Victoria Skating Rink in Montreal. About 18 years later, teams from the **Amateur** Hockey Association of Canada began competing for the **Stanley Cup**, called the Dominion Hockey Challenge Cup at the time. In 1914, the Stanley Cup became the exclusive trophy of two **professional** leagues. These leagues were the National Hockey Association (NHA) and the Pacific Coast Hockey Association (PCHA).

Three years later, the National Hockey League (NHL) was formed out of the NHA. The teams playing in the league at that time were the Montreal Canadiens, the Montreal Wanderers, the Toronto Arenas, and the Ottawa Senators.

■ The Stanley Cup was donated by Lord Stanley, who was governor general of Canada from 1888 to 1893.

4

er the next 25 years, several other
ms joined and left the NHL. When the
eat Depression occurred in the 1930s,
e Montreal Maroons, the New York
nericans, and the original Ottawa
nators withdrew from the league due to
ack of funds. The remaining six teams
the league at the start of the 1942–43
ason became known as the Original Six.
r the next 25 years, no new teams were
owed into the league, and none of the
teams changed locations. In 1967,
e NHL expanded by adding six new
nchises. Since that time, the league
s expanded many times.

day, there are 30 teams in the NHL.
x are based in Canadian cities, and
e other 24 are in the United States.
e Canadian NHL teams are the
ncouver Canucks, the Edmonton
lers, the Calgary Flames, the Toronto
aple Leafs, the Montreal Canadiens,
d the Ottawa Senators.

THE ORIGINAL SIX

Between the 1942–43 season and the
league's expansion in 1967, there were only
six teams in the NHL. They were the
Montreal Canadiens, the Toronto Maple
Leafs, the Detroit Red Wings, the Chicago
Blackhawks, the New York Rangers, and
the Boston Bruins. They are known as the
Original Six.

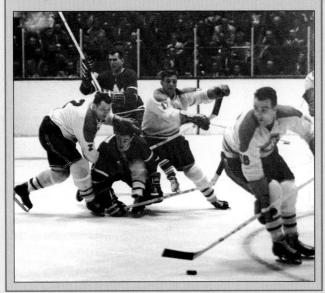

CHANGES THROUGHOUT THE YEARS

PAST	The puck was wooden.	There were seven players per team on the ice.	Forward passes were against the rules.	There were goal posts, but no nets. Goals were scored from either side of the goal line.
PRESENT	The puck is rubber.	There are six players per team on the ice.	Forward passes are allowed.	Nets are used.

The Rise of the Toronto Maple Leafs

1917

The National Hockey League is formed. The first four teams are the Ottawa Senators, the Montreal Wanderers, the Toronto Arenas, and the Montreal Canadiens. The Arenas received their name because their arena was the largest in Toronto. It was also the only one with artificial ice. The Mutual Street Arena is located on Mutual Street between Dundas and Shuter. The team's logo was a big white T.

1918

The Toronto Arenas become the first NHL team to win the Stanley Cup. They defeat the Vancouver Millionaires of the PCHA in a best-of-five series.

1919

The team changes its name from the Arenas to the St. Patricks. Their new jerseys are green and white with the name St. Pats across the front. St. Patrick was an Irish Saint. The name represents the large Irish population living in Toronto at the time.

1922

The Toronto St. Patricks win the Stanley Cup. They defeat the Vancouver Millionaires three games to two. The final game marks the last time NHL teams play with seven players on the ice.

1926

Conn Smythe purchases the team. He changes their name to the Toronto Maple Leafs.

1931

The Maple Leafs move from the Mutual Street Arena to Maple Leaf Garden.

heir first game in the new uilding is on November 12, 931, against the Chicago lackhawks. The Blackhawks eat the Maple Leafs 2–1. fter an up-and-down eason, the Leafs go on o win the Stanley Cup.

952

On November 1, 1952, *Hockey Night in Canada* roadcasts the first Maple Leafs game via television. oster Hewitt announces he game from Maple Leaf Gardens. He ushers hockey fans into the era of elevision with his familiar Hello, Canada!" The elevision show becomes national institution.

961

The Hockey Hall of Fame opens in Toronto.

967

The Toronto Maple Leafs win he Stanley Cup. They defeat he Montreal Canadiens to win the series. This is the fifteenth time the Leafs have won the Cup. It is the last year of the Original Six era. After this, winning the Cup will become more difficult due to the expansion of he league.

1968

Six new NHL teams join the league. They are the California Seals, the St. Louis Blues, the Minnesota North Stars, the Philadelphia Flyers, the Pittsburgh Penguins, and the Los Angeles Kings.

February 7, 1976

Maple Leafs forward Darryl Sittler records 10 points in a single game. Playing at home in Maple Leaf Gardens, Sittler made six goals and four assists in an 11–4 win over the Boston Bruins. This NHL record still stands today.

February 19, 1999

The Maple Leafs move from Maple Leaf Gardens to their new arena, the Air Canada Centre. It is located on Bay Street. After they advance to the Eastern Conference finals, they lose to the Buffalo Sabres.

2005–2006

For the first time since 1998, the Leafs do not make the **playoffs**.

Quick Facts

- Toronto's nickname is "Hogtown." In the early 1900s, many people in the city worked for pork packing plants.
- The CN Tower in Toronto is the tallest freestanding structure in the world.
- Toronto's Yonge Street is the longest street in the world.
- Toronto is home to the third-largest film industry in North America. It follows behind Los Angeles and New York.
- There are 386 parks within Toronto's city limits.
- More than 21 million travellers pass through Toronto's Lester B. Pearson International Airport every year.

Home of the Maple Leafs

The home arena for the Maple Leafs from 1931 to 1999 was Maple Leaf Gardens. The arena could seat 12,000 fans at that time. Over the years, the arena added about 4,000 more seats. The Leafs' first game in the Gardens was against the Chicago Blackhawks. From 1946 to 1999, every Maple Leafs home game in the Gardens was sold out.

During the Maple Leafs' 68-year history, the team has won 11 Stanley Cups and numerous league championships in the Maple Leaf Gardens. Maple Leaf Gardens has hosted many other events. The first NHL All-Star Game was held there in 1934. The Beatles played at the Gardens on three separate occasions. It was also the site of many professional wrestling bouts.

▪▪ The Air Canada Centre can host a Raptors basketball game in the afternoon and be ready for a hockey game four to six hours later.

8

he Maple Leafs played in the Gardens for
he last time in 1999. Like their first game in
he Gardens more than 25 years before, the
Maple Leafs played the Chicago Blackhawks.
he Maple Leafs lost 6–2. Bob Probert of the
lackhawks scored the last NHL goal in
he Gardens.

he Maple Leafs' new home is called Air
anada Centre. The Centre is located in
owntown Toronto. It has a seating capacity
f more than 20,000 fans.

he Maple Leafs played their first home game
the Centre against the Montreal Canadiens
n February 20, 1999. Toronto won 3–2 in
vertime. The Toronto Raptors played their
rst basketball game the following night.
his was the Centre's second official
pening game. The night after the
aptors' game, the Canadian band The
ragically Hip performed the first concert
the Centre. The concert was sold out.

About the Mascot

Carlton the Bear is the Toronto Maple
Leafs' mascot. He is a 6-foot-6-inch polar
bear. He is named after the street where
the Maple Leaf Gardens is located. Carlton
was named to keep the tradition of the
Gardens alive. He has thrown more than
8,000 t-shirts into the audience and has led
the fans in many cheers. Carlton sometimes
attends Maple Leafs games in other cities.
He enjoys travelling to Ottawa. This is
because Spartacat, the Senators mascot,
is his biggest **rival**.

■ Air Canada Centre is also home to the
Toronto Raptors of the National Basketball
Association (NBA).

9

Hockey Positions

The positions in hockey are forward, defence, and goaltender. Each team is allowed six players on the ice. Teams usually play with three forwards, two defencemen, and one goaltender. The forwards include a right winger, left winger, and centre. The defensive pair is a right defender and a left defender.

The main job of all three forwards is to pass the puck up the ice and score goals. The centre generally

takes the **face-off**. The right winger usually stays along the boards on the right side of the rink. The left winger does the same along the left side. The centre generally plays between the two wingers and follows the puck. Darryl Sittler and Dave Keon were two very successful forwards with the Maple Leafs. Sittler collected 916 points while playing for Toronto, the most by any player on the team. Sittler also has the most goals with 389. Keon was second with 858 points and 365 goals. Mats Sundin, the team's current captain, is closing in on Sittler and Keon in both points and goals.

Defencemen try to prevent the **opposition** from scoring goals. They do this by staying between their goalie and the opposing players. They also force the opposition players out of good shooting positions whenever possible. Some defenders score goals and create scoring chances for their forwards. This type of defender is called an

MAPLE LEAFS ALL-TIME LEADERS

Most Goals Darryl Sittler 389 goals	**Most Games Played** George Armstrong 1187 games played
Most Assists Borje Salming 620 assists	**Most Penalty Minutes** Tie Domi 2156 **penalty** minutes
Most Points Darryl Sittler 916 points	**Most Goaltender Wins** Walter Broda 302 wins

offensive defenceman. Borje Salming was a defenceman for Toronto between 1973 and 1989. He scored 148 goals and had 620 assists. The other type of defender is a stay-at-home defenceman, such as Aki Berg. Stay-at-home defencemen rarely race up ice with the puck. Instead, they stay close to their goalie to prevent the other team from scoring.

The goalie's job is to stop the opposition from scoring. Goalies are the last line of defence. If they miss the puck, a goal is scored. Over the years, some of the NHL's best goalies have played for Toronto. Walter "Turk" Broda leads the team with 629 games played and 302 wins. He is followed by Johnny Bower and Felix Potvin. Goaltender Ed Belfour won the Calder Trophy as the best first-year player, two Vezina Trophies as the league's top goalie, and four William M. Jennings Trophies for the lowest goals against average. He also won a Stanley Cup with the Dallas Stars in 1999.

■ In 2006, Mikael Tellqvist set the record for the least playtime in an NHL game, playing only 0.5 seconds.

The Goalie and his mask

Mike Palmateer was a goalie with Toronto in the late 1970s and early 1980s. Masks at that time were different than they are today. They were made of fibreglass and were one piece. They were moulded to the goalie's face for a tight fit. Palmateer's mask was white with blue maple leafs. His jersey number was painted on top.

Trevor Kidd played for the Maple Leafs from 2002 to 2004. The design on his mask was painted to match the team's colours. It featured a white maple leaf on the chin with "Kidder 37" written on it. Flames flared along each side. A skull was painted on the forehead.

Goalies often express themselves through special designs on their masks. Ed Belfour's nickname is "Eddie the Eagle." He has eagles painted on his mask. When Belfour played for the the Maple Leafs, his mask was mainly blue and white. These colours show Eddie the Eagle's pride in playing for the Maple Leafs.

Hockey Equipment

Hockey is a fast, rough sport. Players wear padded equipment to prevent injuries. Hockey equipment is like body armor. It includes helmets, padded gloves, knee-length padded pants, and loose, stretchy jerseys. Each jersey has the player's last name and number on the back.

Players also wear shoulder pads, elbow pads, and thick socks with shin pads underneath. Some players wear a visor on their helmets to protect their eyes. Other players do not. In 2006, Mats Sundin of the Maple Leafs suffered a serious eye injury because he was not wearing a visor. This injury caused him to miss many games. When he returned, he wore a visor until his eye was healed. Today's skates are made of leather and various plastic materials. These new skates are designed to be light. They allow players to turn more sharply and skate faster than they did before. Players have their skate blades sharpened many times throughout the season.

HELMET

VISOR

SHOULDER PADS

ELBOW PADS

GLOVES

HOCKEY STICK

PANTS

SHIN PADS

SKATES

12

altenders wear special equipment to
tect them from hard shots fired at them.
ne players can fire the puck faster than
) kilometres per hour.

altenders wear thick pads that reach from
ir thighs to their skates. They use these
ls to deflect the puck away from their net.
ey also wear a catcher or trapper on one
nd and a blocker on the other. A goalie's
cher is similar to a baseball glove. The
cker is a glove attached to a long, flat,
lded surface. Goalies use the blocker to
lect the puck into the corner, away from
net.

Team Jerseys

In the past, all hockey games were played on outdoor rinks. Players wore turtleneck sweaters and knitted wool caps to keep warm. Today, teams wear matching jerseys bearing their team logo.

The Toronto Arenas franchise began play in the 1917–18 season. They had no official name at that time. Fans began calling them the Blue Shirts because of the blue jerseys they wore. In their second season, the team officially became known as the Toronto Arenas. They continued to wear the blue jerseys, but they added a large T on the front. The T represented Toronto.

In 1919, the franchise was rescued from bankruptcy. The owners wanted to give the Toronto St. Patricks a new start. They changed the team's colours to green and white.

Today, the Toronto Maple Leafs have three jerseys. Their home jersey is blue with white trim. These colours represent Canada's blue sky and snowy winters. Their away jersey is white with blue trim. The team's logo is a maple leaf with their name written inside the leaf. The Maple Leafs wear their third jersey only on special occasions. It has a stylized maple leaf on the front.

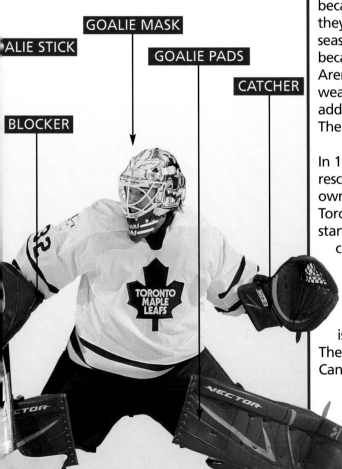

GOALIE MASK

ALIE STICK

GOALIE PADS

CATCHER

BLOCKER

Competing in the National Hockey League

There are currently 30 teams in the National Hockey League. Half of the teams play in the Eastern Conference. The other half play in the Western Conference. Each conference is made up of three divisions. In the Eastern Conference, the divisions include the Atlantic Division, the Northeast Division, and the Southeast Division, while in the Western Conference, the Central Division, the Northwest Division, and the Pacific Division are included.

Eight teams from each conference advance from the regular season to the playoffs. Playoff spots in the conference quarter finals are awarded on the basis of points earned during the regula season. Teams are **seeded** from #1 to based on their regular-season poin Four series are then played with # playing #8, #2 playing #7, and so Each series is a best-of-seven format The first team to win four games wins the series.

Winners of the conference quarter finals advance to the conference semifinals. The winning teams a then seeded in each series, base on the same criteria as the quart finals. Winners of the semifinal series then advance to the conference finals. Conference winners play each other for the Stanley Cup.

■ The Maple Leafs have won the Stanley Cup 11 times.

WESTERN CONFERENCE

Central Division	Northwest Division	Pacific Division
CHICAGO BLACKHAWKS	🍁CALGARY FLAMES	ANAHEIM DUCKS
COLUMBUS BLUE JACKETS	COLORADO AVALANCHE	DALLAS STARS
DETROIT RED WINGS	🍁EDMONTON OILERS	LOS ANGELES KINGS
NASHVILLE PREDATORS	MINNESOTA WILD	PHOENIX COYOTES
ST. LOUIS BLUES	🍁VANCOUVER CANUCKS	SAN JOSE SHARKS

WESTERN CONFERENCE

QUARTER FINALS

| #1 versus #8 | #2 versus #7 |
| #3 versus #6 | #4 versus #5 |

Top four teams move to next round

| #1 versus #4 |
| #2 versus #3 |

SEMIFINALS

Top two teams move to next round

| #1 versus #2 |

CONFERENCE FINALS

Top team moves to last round

Top in West → Versus ← Top in East

Top team moves to last round

↓

Stanley Cup Champion

EASTERN CONFERENCE

QUARTER FINALS

| #1 versus #8 | #2 versus #7 |
| #3 versus #6 | #4 versus #5 |

Top four teams move to next round

| #1 versus #4 |
| #2 versus #3 |

Top two teams move to next round

| #1 versus #2 |

EASTERN CONFERENCE

Atlantic Division
NEW JERSEY DEVILS
NEW YORK ISLANDERS
NEW YORK RANGERS
PHILADELPHIA FLYERS
PITTSBURGH PENGUINS

Northeast Division
BOSTON BRUINS
BUFFALO SABRES
🍁 MONTREAL CANADIENS
🍁 OTTAWA SENATORS
🍁 TORONTO MAPLE LEAFS

Southeast Division
ATLANTA THRASHERS
CAROLINA HURRICANES
FLORIDA PANTHERS
TAMPA BAY LIGHTNING
WASHINGTON CAPITALS

The Battle of Ontario

The Toronto Maple Leafs play in the Northeast Division of the Eastern Conference. They compete with the other teams in the conference for a playoff position. Their biggest rival in their division is the Ottawa Senators. This is because more than just a playoff position is at stake when these two teams meet.

Bragging rights for the province are also on the line.

This rivalry has become known as the Battle of Ontario. The two teams compete as hard as possible when playing each other. This sometimes causes rivalries to develop between individual players. Some individual battles can last for years.

arcy Tucker of the Maple Leafs and Chris
eil of the Senators have been battling each
her for years. In the 2004 playoffs, their
attle reached an all-time high. The Maple
eafs were winning the final game of the
ries. Just before the end of the game, Tucker
aved goodbye to Neil, indicating that the
enators were abut to be eliminated from the
ayoffs. Neil was furious.

he Battle of Ontario is one of the best
valries in hockey. So far, the Maple Leafs
ave won the majority of the battles. They
ave defeated the Senators in the three playoff
ries that the two teams have played against
ch other.

The Battle of the Fans

There are many Toronto Maple Leafs fans
across Canada. This is because the Maple
Leafs have been around for a long time.
There are even some Maple Leafs fans in
Ottawa. These fans became loyal to the
Maple Leafs when Ottawa did not have a
team. Most people in Ottawa now cheer for
the Senators, but some fans still cheer for
the Maple Leafs. Radio stations, newspapers,
and fans in both cities gloat whenever their
team wins.

Making It to the NHL

Each year in June, the National Hockey League has a draft. It is called the NHL **Entry Draft**. During the Entry Draft, NHL teams select players from the Canadian Hockey League (CHL) and various **semi-professional** leagues around the world to play on their team. Teams that finish low in the NHL regular season standings select first. Teams that finish high in the standings select last. This order helps balance the talent pool in the league.

Many players that are drafted have played in the Canadian Hockey League (CHL). The CHL is a junior league made up of players between the ages of 16 to 20. Sometimes drafted players are returned to the CHL to further develop their skills. Kyle Wellwood of the Maple Leafs was drafted in the fifth round in 2001. He spent the next few seasons developing his skills with the St. John's Leafs of the American Hockey League (AHL) and the Windsor Spitfires of the CHL. Bryan McCabe also played in the CHL before making it to the NHL.

Some NHL hockey players are traded to different teams in exchange for other players. They may also be traded for draft choices.

▪▪ The 24th pick in the 2002 NHL Entry Draft, Alexander Steen, had 45 points for the Leafs in his rookie season.

Mats Sundin, a centre with the Maple Leafs, was acquired by the team in a trade with the Quebec Nordiques. He had been drafted by the Nordiques first overall in the 1989 NHL Entry Draft.

NHL team **rosters** are made up of signed players. NHL teams sign the players that they think will give them the best chance of winning. Signed players may be sent to the AHL for a while. The AHL is a semi-professional league. Most NHL franchises own an AHL team. Toronto's AHL affiliate team is the Toronto Marlies. Players that are too old to play in the CHL are often sent to the AHL to develop their skills. Some players play for years in the AHL before having an opportunity to play in the NHL. After the Maple Leafs drafted Wellwood, he played for one year in the CHL and then two seasons in the AHL. In 2005, he joined the Maple Leafs as a rookie centre. Wellwood is considered to be one of the Maple Leafs' budding young stars.

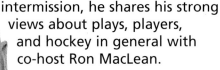

Reporting on the Maple Leafs

Hockey Night in Canada

Hockey Night in Canada began broadcasting on CBC radio in Toronto in the 1930s. Foster Hewitt did the play-by-play commentary. He was Canada's voice of hockey on radio and television for more than 60 years. He coined the phrase, "He shoots! He scores!" When hockey broadcasters are inducted into the Hockey Hall of Fame, they receive the Foster Hewitt Memorial Award.

Today, most hockey fans associate Don Cherry with *Hockey Night in Canada*. Almost every Saturday night since 1980, "Grapes" has entertained and informed fans during Coach's Corner. During intermission, he shares his strong views about plays, players, and hockey in general with co-host Ron MacLean.

The Olympics

Canadian Olympic Men's Hockey

The Canadian Olympic Men's hockey team is made up of the best hockey players of Canadian citizenship. NHL hockey fans from across the country cheer for them in the Olympics. The Canadian team's main rivals are Russia, the United States, the Czech Republic, Finland, and Sweden. Since 1920, Canada has won seven gold medals in Olympic hockey.

In the past, NHL players were not able to compete in the Winter Olympics. Canada would send amateur players to the games. In 1998, NHL players began to play on Canada's Olympic hockey team. Canada failed to capture a medal that year in Nagano, Japan. This was very disappointing for the team and for hockey fans across Canada. In 2002, Team Canada captured the gold medal in Salt Lake City, Utah. They defeated the United States in the gold medal game. Hockey fans from across Canada were delighted by the victory. Curtis Joseph, the Maple Leafs' goaltender at the time, was the third goalie for Team Canada.

■ As a member of Team Canada, former Leafs goaltender Curtis Joseph played in five games at the 2002 Olympics. Team Canada won a gold medal.

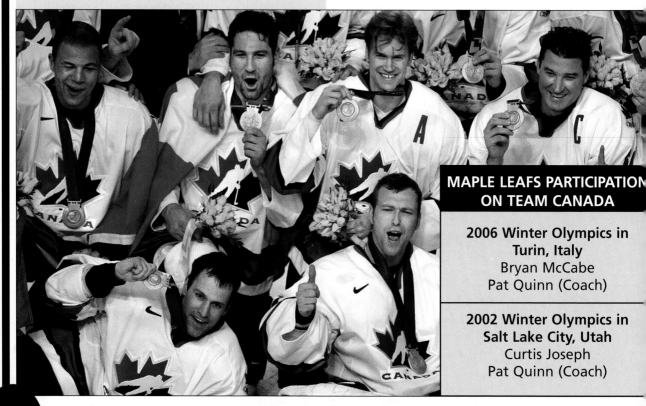

MAPLE LEAFS PARTICIPATION ON TEAM CANADA

2006 Winter Olympics in Turin, Italy
Bryan McCabe
Pat Quinn (Coach)

2002 Winter Olympics in Salt Lake City, Utah
Curtis Joseph
Pat Quinn (Coach)

anadian Olympic Women's Hockey

he Canadian Olympic Women's hockey team
gan competing in the Winter Olympics in
998. Their team is made up of players from
e National Women's Hockey League
IWHL). The Canadian women's team's
ggest international rival is the United States.
1998, Canada lost to the United States in
e gold medal game. Hockey fans in Canada
ere devastated. However, Canada beat the
S. team in the gold medal round in 2002 in
lt Lake City, Utah. Then, in 2006, they beat
veden in Turin, Italy, to again capture the
ld medal. The team has been led by star
rwards Cassie Campbell and Hayley
ickenheiser. Wickenheiser is the only
oman to ever score a goal in a professional
en's hockey league game.

■ The Canadian Olympic Women's hockey team
outscored their opponents 28–0 in their first
two round robin games of the 2006 Olympics
in Turin Italy.

21

Popular Maple Leafs Coaches

George "Punch" Imlach

With just a month into the 1958–59 season, the last-place Maple Leafs showed few signs of improvement. Punch Imlach took over as coach and promised that the sixth-place team would be in the playoffs by the end of the season. Most people laughed. With three games left, the Maple Leafs trailed the New York Rangers by five points. In one of the most incredible finishes of all time, Toronto won all three of its games, and the Rangers lost all of their games. Imlach's prediction had come true. During the next 10 years, the team won four Stanley Cups with Imlach as coach. He built up the franchise by adding **veteran** players to the roster, sometimes giving up promising young talent. He worked his teams hard and criticized players when they made a bad play. Many players on the team did not like the way he treated them. Imlach coached the Maple Leafs for 760 games. During that time, the Leafs recorded 365 wins and 125 ties.

Mike Murphy

Mike Murphy spent 12 hockey seasons playing for the St. Louis Blues, the New York Rangers, and the Los Angeles Kings. After retiring as a player, he moved into coaching the Los Angeles Kings. Then in 1991, he became an assistant coach with the Maple Leafs. He helped coach the Maple Leafs for the next three years. He then joined the New York Rangers as an assistant coach. After two years with the Rangers, Murphy rejoined the Maple Leafs as the head coach. He coached the Maple Leafs for 164 games, recording 60 wins and 17 ties. When he left the Leafs in 1998, he helped coach the Ottawa Senators. In 1999, the NHL offered Murphy the position of vice president of hockey operations for the league, a position he still holds today.

Pat Quinn

In 1978, Pat Quinn landed his first NHL head coaching job with the Philadelphia Flyers. In the next season, he won the Jack Adams Award. This trophy is awarded to the best NHL coach each year. Later, Quinn coached the Kings and the Vancouver Canucks. In the 1991–92 season, he won the Jack Adams Award for a second time. Only two other coaches have won the Jack Adams

ward with two different teams. In his
unger years, Pat Quinn played for two
asons with the Toronto Maple Leafs. In
98, he returned to the team as the head
ach. He continued in this position until
06. He guided the Maple Leafs to the
Eastern Conference finals three times.
In 2002, Quinn had also coached
the Canadian Olympic Men's
hockey team to a gold medal in
the Winter Olympics in Salt
Lake City, Utah. He also
coached Team Canada in 2006.

Making the Call

As well as coaches and players, the NHL
needs game officials. Game officials are
linesmen and referees. Linesmen call
offsides and **icing,** while referees call most
of the penalties. Referees need to be good
skaters because they have to keep up with
the play for an entire game. Unlike hockey
players, referees are not able to rest
between **shifts**.

Referees are so important to hockey that
several have been inducted into the Hockey
Hall of Fame. You can read about them on
the Hockey Hall of Fame website at
www.legendsofhockey.net.

The first step to becoming a referee is to
contact a local league office. Training is
available at officiating schools, such as the
North American School of Officiating in
Guelph, Ontario. These schools teach ice
positioning, signals, penalty calling,
skating skills, and off-ice theory.

A referee needs all of these skills so
that he or she can make the right
calls during a game. Every year,
referees attend a week-long
training camp. During the camp,
fitness level and skating ability are
tested. At the end of the week,
referees leave camp and head to
their first game of the season.

Unforgettable Moments

The Toronto Maple Leafs have a long history, and there have been many unforgettable moments. One such event is the Maple Leafs' Stanley Cup victory in 1967. The Leafs and the Montreal Canadiens faced off in the Stanley Cup finals. The Maple Leafs defeated the Canadiens in this historic series. This marked the end of the Original Six era. The next season, the league expanded to 12 teams.

Darryl Sittler, a centre with the team, was involved in several memorable events. On February 7, 1976, in a game against the Boston Bruins, Sittler recorded 6 goals and assists for 10 points. This is an NHL record that still stands today. Just two months later Sittler scored five goals in a playoff game against the Philadelphia Flyers.

Many fans fondly remember the time Doug Gilmour scored a wraparound goal to end the second-longest game in Maple Leafs history. was the 1993 playoffs, and the Maple Leafs and St. Louis Blues were playing each other the first game of the division finals.

■ Ed Belfour was the Leafs goaltender during their 2004 playoff series win over Ottawa. Belfour is second in All-time NHL wins with 457.

oug Gilmour got the puck behind the Blues
et. He faked that he was going to take the
uck to his left. Then he spun around and
ked to his right. Finally, he came around the
ght side of the net and shot the puck past
e goalie. It was three minutes and 16
conds into the second overtime period.

The Maple Leafs 2004 playoff victory against the Ottawa Senators was celebrated by Leafs' fans flying flags and honking horns. The battle of Ontario had been won once again by the Maple Leafs.

NHL INDIVIDUAL AND TEAM AWARDS WON BY THE MAPLE LEAFS

Name of Award	Awarded to	Leafs Winners
rank J. Selke Trophy	the best **defensive forward**	Doug Gilmour, 1993
ing Clancy Award	the player who demonstrates strong leadership skills on and off the ice	Curtis Joseph, 2000
ezina Trophy	the best goalie	Johnny Bower, 1961 Johnny Bower and Terry Sawchuk, 1965
onn Smythe Trophy	the most valuable player during the playoffs	Dave Keon, 1967
ady Byng Trophy	the player who best combines hockey skill, sportsmanship, and gentlemanly conduct	Red Kelly, 1961 Dave Keon, 1962 Dave Keon, 1963 Alexander Mogilny, 2003
alder Trophy	the best rookie, or first-year player	Dave Keon, 1961 Kent Douglas, 1963 Brit Selby, 1966
ack Adams Award	the coach deemed most influential to the team's success	Pat Burns, 1993

25

Maple Leafs Legends and Current Stars

#14 Dave Keon

CAREER FACTS

Dave Keon began to play for the Toronto Maple Leafs in the fall of 1960, when he was only 19 years old. Keon used bursts of speed and quick moves around the net. He had a powerful backhand shot that fooled goaltenders. Keon won the Calder Trophy in 1961 and played a major role in the Maple Leafs' four Stanley Cup wins during the 1960s. He was the most valuable player (MVP) of the playoffs in 1967 and won the Conn Smythe Trophy.

Position Centre
Born March 22, 1940

Hometown
Rouyn-Noranda, Quebec

#39 Doug Gilmour

CAREER FACTS

Doug Gilmour was drafted by the St. Louis Blues in 1982. During his NHL career, he played for the Blues, Calgary Flames, Toronto Maple Leafs, New Jersey Devils, Chicago Blackhawks, Buffalo Sabres, and Montreal Canadiens. In 1,474 career NHL games, he recorded 450 goals and 964 assists. Gilmour was known for his playmaking ability. In 1990–91, he was part of one of the biggest hockey trades in NHL history. He was traded from the Calgary Flames to the Toronto Maple Leafs in a 10-player deal. In 1992–93, Gilmour recorded 127 regular season points with Toronto. This is a Maple Leafs record, and it won him the Selke Trophy as the top defensive forward.

Position Centre
Born June 25, 1963

Hometown
Kingston, Ontario

#27 Darryl Sittler

CAREER FACTS

The Maple Leafs made Darryl Sittler the eighth pick overall in the 1970 NHL Entry Draft. He quickly established himself as an offensive star. Sittler took over the captain's duties at 24 years of age—the second-youngest captain in Maple Leafs history. Sittler had an incredible year in 1975–76. He became the first Maple Leafs player to reach 100 points in a season. During the **Canada Cup**, he scored an overtime goal against Czechoslovakia to win the Cup for Canada. Sittler was a Canadian hero.

Position Centre
Born September 18, 1950

Hometown
Kitchener, Ontario

When Ed Belfour was the Maple Leafs' goalie, he said this about the team's struggles in 2006: "That's just the way it goes sometimes. I've been through it before. All the guys on the team have been through things like this before. We have to keep working hard, not give up, and stay with the plan."

Mats Sundin said this about winning a gold medal with Sweden at the 2006 Winter Olympics in Turin, Italy: "It's an amazing feeling. ...To win gold with this team, and for the Swedish people, is an honour."

#13 Mats Sundin

CAREER FACTS

In 1989, Mats Sundin was drafted first overall by the Quebec Nordiques. He was then traded from the Nordiques to the Maple Leafs in 1994. Sundin is known as a **power forward** because he combines size and strength with skill. Sundin is also a good playmaker. Opposing players have difficulty knocking him off the puck. In 1,137 career NHL games to the end of the 2005–06 season, Sundin has recorded 496 goals and 671 assists, for 1,167 points. Sundin is the Maple Leafs captain.

Position Centre
Born February 13, 1971

Hometown
Bromma, Sweden

The Best Years

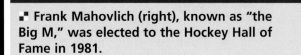

■ Frank Mahovlich (right), known as "the Big M," was elected to the Hockey Hall of Fame in 1981.

The Toronto Maple Leafs have won the Stanley Cup 11 times. Only the Montreal Canadiens have won more Stanley Cups than the Maple Leafs. The Canadiens have won it 24 times.

The Maple Leafs were very successful between 1947 and 1951. They won the Stanley Cup in 1947, 1948, and 1949. This was the first time an NHL team had won the Stanley Cup three years in a row. After losing in the first round in the 1949–50 season, the Maple Leafs rebounded to reclaim the Stanley Cup the following year. That year they were led by Max Bentley and Bill Barilko. In game five of a best-of-five series, Bentley scored the tying goal with 32 seconds left in the third period. The game went to overtime. Barilko, who had only six goals during the regular season, scored to become an unlikely hero. The Maple Leafs won their fourth Stanley Cup in five years.

The Leafs again won the Stanley Cup three years in a row from 1962 to 1964. This time they were led by a number of hockey legends. These included Frank Mahovlich, Red

ly, Johnny Bower, Dave Keon, Andy
hgate, and Tim Horton. Today, all of
se players are in the Hockey Hall
Fame.

e Maple Leafs' last Stanley Cup
tory was in 1967. They defeated
Montreal Canadiens in six
nes. This was a special victory for
ny reasons. First, the Canadiens
re expected to win the series. As well,
ve Keon captured the Conn Smythe
ophy as the best player in the playoffs.

r the next 20 years, the Maple Leafs
nained competitive, but they were not
ampions. The team re-emerged in the 1990s
h new ownership. To regain its competitive
rit, the team traded for Doug Gilmour.
mour quickly became a fan favourite. He
o became one of the best players on the
m. In 1993, Gilmour recorded 127 points
lead the Maple Leafs in scoring. The team
ished the regular season with 44 wins, 29
ses, and 11 ties, for 99 points. This remains
ir best regular-season finish in franchise
tory. In the playoffs, they advanced to the
nference finals. Since 1993, they have
de it to the Conference finals three
nes and have only missed the
yoffs twice.

MAPLE LEAFS IN THE COMMUNITY

The Toronto Maple Leafs have a
special organization called the
Leafs Fund. The Leafs Fund
raises money to help
children participate in
extra-curricular activities.
This organization has
raised thousands of dollars
to date. One of the Leafs
Fund events is a 50/50 draw
at each Maple Leafs home
game. Half of the money from
this draw is used to fund the Leafs
Dreams Youth Arts Scholarship
Program and the Send a
Kid to Camp Program.

Every year the Maple
Leafs visit the
Hospital for Sick
Children in Toronto.
This gives the
children at the
hospital an
opportunity to meet
their heroes. On December
7, 2004, the entire team and
coaching staff visited the hospital. They
signed autographs, told stories, and Carlton
the Bear gave each child a Christmas gift.

Tie Domi, a former Maple Leaf
winger, was very involved in
the community. Every year
during Christmas, Domi
dressed up like Santa
Claus and invited 100
children to attend a
Christmas Party at the Air
Canada Centre. He signed
autographs, handed out
Christmas gifts, and invited
the guests to attend a Maple
Leafs practice.

29

Quiz

1 Where and when was the first hockey game played?

2 How many teams play in the NHL?

3 When did the NHL begin?

4 What is the name of the Maple Leafs' home arena?

5 Who became the coach of the Maple Leafs in 1998?

6 Who is the only woman to ever score a goal in a professional men's hockey league game?

7 Which year was the Maple Leafs most recent Stanley Cup win?

8 Who are the Maple Leafs biggest rivals during the past 10 years?

9 Who has scored the most goals as a Maple Leafs player?

10 Which member of the Maple Leafs wa. part of Team Canada at th. 2006 Winter Olympics?

nswers

The first hockey game was ...ayed at the Victoria Skating ...k in Montreal in 1875.
Thirty teams play in the NHL.
The NHL began in 1917.
The Maple Leafs' home arena ...the Air Canada Centre.
Pat Quinn became coach ... 1998.
Hayley Wickenheiser is the ...ly woman to score a goal ...a professional men's ...ockey league.
The Maple Leafs won the ...anley Cup in 1967.
The Ottawa Senators are the ...aple Leafs' biggest rivals.
Darryl Sittler has scored ...e most goals as a Maple ...afs player.
. Bryan McCabe was a member ... Team Canada.

Further Research

e Toronto Maple Leafs were one of the Original Six teams in the NHL. Many books and
bsites have been established to provide information on the Maple Leafs. To learn more
ut them, borrow books from the library, or surf the Internet.

— BOOKS TO READ —

st libraries have computers that connect to a database for researching information.
ou input a key word, you will be provided with a list of books in the library that
tain information on that topic. Non-fiction books are arranged numerically, using
ir call number. Fiction books are organized alphabetically by the author's last name.

find books about the Toronto Maple Leafs, type key words such as
ronto Maple Leafs" or "NHL teams" into the search field.

— ONLINE SITES —

http://sports.espn.go.com/nhl/
clubhouse?team=tor

www.mapleleafs.com

http://sportsillustrated.cnn.com/
hockey/nhl/teams/maple_leafs/

31

Glossary

amateur: a player who is not a professional and plays a sport for the pleasure of it without being paid money to play

Canada Cup: a hockey tournament featuring the best players in the world representing their countries

defensive forward: a player who checks the opposition's best player to prevent them from scoring a goal

entry draft: a process used by NHL teams to select new players

face-off: when the referee drops the puck between two players to start the play

franchises: teams or organizations that become members of a league

Great Depression: the time between 1929 and 1934 when business was bad and many people lost their jobs

Hockey Hall of Fame: a place where former players and people involved in hockey are honored for their contributions to the game

icing: a stoppage in play caused by a player shooting the puck from his or her side of the centre line to the opposition's goal line without it being touched

offsides: stops in play caused by a player crossing the offensive blue line before the puck

opposition: a team that opposes another team

penalty: a punishment for breaking a rule of the game

playoffs: a final game or series of games played to decide who will be champion

power forward: a forward who combines skill and toughness

professional: earning a living from a sport

rival: a competitor

rosters: lists of players playing on teams

seeded: being placed in a specific rank or position

semi-professional: a player who plays for money, but is paid less than what professionals are paid

shifts: groups of players taking turns with other groups of players while playing a game

Stanley Cup: the National Hockey League's prize for the best team in the playoffs

veteran: a player who has considerable experience playing in the NHL

Index

My dress will be amazing.

The world's smoothest silk

Really rare diamonds

Princess lives here

I'm a princess... you may curtsy!

A thou...
p...

I will have a new dress made for the ball.

This lady is fantastic at making pretty clothes.

My new dress

Party princess

On my birthday, I will have a ball (a really BIG party).

My favorite pet will be my magical unicorn.

I will have lots of royal pets to play with.

Princess's pet corner

Prize-
winning
puppy →

I will be able to eat anything I want.

Pancakes

Ice cream

chocolate sauce

Pampered princess

I will choose my meals from a royal menu.

Food fit for a princess

List of my favorite breakfasts

Royal menu

Royal cereal

She will even use magic to help me get dressed.

"Hmm . . . I think I'll wear the pink dress today."

"No Problem!"

"Just call me PRINCESS"

My Fairy Godmother will wake me up every morning.

"Good morning, Princess."

She will cast a magic spell to make the sun shine.

But my bedroom will be the best room of all.

Six extra-squishy pillows

Four mattresses (great for bouncing)

The palace will have hundreds of rooms.

REALLY big closet

One day I will be a Princess.

My mom
(the queen)

My dad
(the king)

Me

I'm going to be the best princess ever!

PaRRagon

Bath · New York · Singapore · Hong Kong · Cologne · Delhi · Melbourne

Illustrated by Caroline Davis

Written by Grace Swanton

First published by Parragon in 2008
Parragon
Queen Street House
4 Queen Street
Bath BA1 1HE, UK

ISBN 978-1-4075-1584-7

Printed in China

I will help make the food and drink, too.

Party cake

Fruit punch that I made all by myself

Pizza that I helped make

On my birthday, I will take forever to get ready.

Extra-bubbly bubble bath

Heart-shaped soap

Special princess perfume

My **F**airy **G**odmother will help me look beautiful.

Dream princess

I will wear my favorite jewels.

I will welcome all my guests to the Palace.

The most handsome prince in the world will come.

We will do some ballroom dancing.

We will all dance and dance until midnight.

Everyone will say **I** am the best Princess ever!

Perfect princess! $\longrightarrow$

Pink-loving
Princess